HOW WE UNDERSTAND THE WORLD
Intelligent Machines

ALAN MACFARLANE was born in Shillong, India, in 1941 and educated at the Dragon School, Sedbergh School, Oxford and London Universities. He is the author of over twenty published books, including *The Origins of English Individualism* (1978) and *Letters to Lily: On How the World Works* (2005). He has worked in England, Nepal, Japan and China as both an historian and anthropologist.

He was elected to the British Academy in 1986 and is now Emeritus Professor of Anthropology at the University of Cambridge and a Life Fellow of King's College, Cambridge.

Intelligent Machines
Conversations with Gerry

ALAN MACFARLANE

2018

First published in 2017
Second edition published in 2018

Cam Rivers Publishing
5 Canterbury Close
Cambridge
CB4 3QQ
www.cambridgerivers.com

Series Editor: Zilan Wang
Contact: press@cambridgerivers.com

Typesetting, book and cover design by Jaimie Norman
Assistant Editor Sarah Harrison

Copyright of written content © Alan Macfarlane
Copyright of cover design and typesetting © Cam Rivers Publishing

The Kaifeng Foundation generously supports the publishing of this book

The Moral right of the author has been asserted.

All rights reserved. Without limiting the rights under copyright reserved above, no part of this publication may be reproduced, stored or introduced into a retrieval system, or transmitted, in any form or by any means (electronic, mechanical, photocopying, recording or otherwise), without prior written permission of both the copyright owner and publisher of this book.

Dedicated to Gerry Martin
Alan Macfarlane 2017

Contents

PREFACE: *Intelligent Machines*   9

1 How and Why Technologies Develop   14

2 Tools of Thought: *Extensions of the Mind to 1936*   25

3 The Era of Intelligent Machines;
Developments Since 1936   33

4 Some Consequences of Technological Change   48

5 Living with Intelligent Machines   66

Preface

Intelligent Machines

THIS BOOK IS dedicated to Gerry Martin who died on 14th January 2004. I worked with Gerry for fourteen years on various intellectual problems and as a retired engineer and industrialist he brought many new ways of thinking to me. He often urged me to write short books summing up my anthropological and historical investigations and it was in response to this that I wrote *Letters to Lily*, which he read, but was unable to see published in 2005. The ideas he gave me of writing simply for a wider audience is behind a series of eight small books I have written over the last few years for young people, and particularly for those in China. In the previous books I have covered many subjects which we discussed. Yet I have realised that there is one large gap, and that is precisely in the area where we did most of our work together.

We worked extensively on some of the consequences of earlier technologies, in particular on glass, on which we wrote a book together, Alan Macfarlane and Gerry Martin, *The Glass Bathyscaphe: How Glass Changed the World* (2002). Important though glass is, I think that if Gerry were still alive he would agree that if we look back over the last fifty thousand years of human history with its many revolutions, and then consider what has happened in the last fifty years and is happening now, we can see that we are on the edge of the greatest change in the experience of *homo sapiens* on this planet. Without being sensational and predicting the demise of *homo sapiens* and his or her replacement by *homo artificilis* (artificial intelligence humans), we can nonetheless see that almost everything in our world is undergoing a huge change.

Whether we consider the professions of law, education, medicine, government, the military, or the jobs people do to produce and distribute goods, we can see enormous changes occurring. Most of us have little understanding of how and why this is happening, so we are not in a position to think rationally about how best to control the new forces we have unleashed.

We are in the situation of the sorcerer's apprentice. The apprentice, while his master was away, remembered one of the spells to activate the brushes and other tools for cleaning the house and fetch water. As they gathered in pace, the tools flew out of his control and he could not halt them. He did not know the counter-spell. We may be in that position now.

We are in the grip of an immense, machine-made, world that is pushing us forwards, driven by a mixture of human curiosity, competitiveness and greed, which it is probably impossible to halt. What was likely to happen was foretold as long ago as 1863 by Samuel Butler in his *Darwin Among the Machines*, where he predicted that machines would displace humans. This may well happen. If we are to avoid this and other negative consequences, we need to understand better what has happened in the past and why it happened. History does not repeat itself, but it rhymes.

Much of what has and is being achieved has been immensely beneficial for humans, but it is also a vast challenge, not just to our jobs but also our ethics, our political systems and our very identities and self-image. We need to understand more about what the phenomena created by intelligent machines means.

* * *

Gerry and I often discussed the meaning of technology and why it seemed to be a particularly developed part of human civilisations. We noticed that the greatest strength of humans is their weakness. Humans are born highly vulnerable and for several years are unable to walk or talk well. Hence we are largely defenceless against predators or other calamities. As we grow into maturity, we lack the specialised parts of the body which give other animals a competitive advantage.

We do not have fur, or at least not much of it, so cannot survive naturally in very cold climates. We do not have feathers so cannot fly. We do not have sharp and strong talons on our feet or hands so cannot rip at plants or animals effectively. We do not have large teeth to attack or chew hard foods. We do not have a large gut which can digest fibrous plants like grass. Our ears are not nearly as acute as those of many animals. Our eyes do not have the telescopic quality of certain birds and mammals. We cannot run very fast. Our arms and backs and legs are not particularly strong.

Yet it is these very absences which have forced us to extend our weak bodies by the use of 'tools', technology, which has ultimately led to our success in the fight for survival. Employing our two outstanding characteristics, delicate and highly flexible hands and fingers, and powerful brains, we define ourselves from others as 'Wise Humans', *Homo Sapiens Sapiens*.

The history of human life on earth over the last fifty thousand years can be written as an account of the increasing power of extensions to our bodies and brains. Many of the extensions to humans over the preceding millennia were to the physical body, though there were parallel developments such as writing, printing and photography which improved our mental power. Now we are at the dawn of an era when machines, another extension of humans, will take over many of the tasks which were traditionally undertaken by humans. It is a huge challenge to all human life and unless we understand what is happening we will not even begin to be able to see how we can control the consequences.

* * *

Gerry and I took a wide definition of technology. As an engineer Gerry knew better than I that technology encompasses not just physical objects, but the skills and knowledge with which they are used. This covers everything from the simplest advances, a better knot, a sharper flint, a more elegant song, through to hugely complicated 'machines', whether a jumbo jet, huge container ships, or the immensely complex airports and harbours which make them possible.

For technology is always about much more than physical things. As Gerry constantly stressed to me, technology is always about embedding knowledge, reliable knowledge, into action, including movement and things. Technology has always reached well beyond the moving of atoms, material inventions, which is why Braudel rightly defines technology so broadly.

Everything is technology: not only man's 'violent exertions' but also his patient and monotonous efforts to make a mark upon the external world; not only the brisk changes we are a little too quick to label revolutions (gunpowder, navigation on the high seas, printing press, wind and water-mills, the first machinery) but also the slow improvements in processes and tools. Technology is also all those innumerable actions which certainly have no innovating significance but which are the fruit of accumulated knowledge: the sailor fixing his ropes, the miner digging his gallery, the peasant behind his plough, the smith at his anvil.

The broad definition of technology which I have adopted here is well expressed by the anthropologist Marcel Mauss. 'I call technique an action which is *effective* and *traditional* (and you will see that in this it is no different from a magical, religious or symbolic action). It has to be *effective* and *traditional*. There is no technique and no transmission in the absence of tradition. This above all is what distinguishes humans from the animals: the transmission of their techniques very probably their oral transmission.'[1] Or again, 'Techniques are to be defined as *traditional actions combined in order to produce a mechanical, physical, or chemical effect, these actions being recognised to have that effect.*'[2]

The tools humans make are always an extension not only of their bodies, but their minds as well. It is essential to grasp this if we are to understand what has happened in the past, why it has happened, and the immense consequences of such technologies in the past, present and future.

---

1 MARCEL MAUSS, *Techniques, Technology and Civilisation* (2006), 82 (Italics in original).
2 MAUSS, *Techniques*, 98

ONE

How and Why Technologies Develop

IN THE PAST, technological evolution in the widest sense proceeded by a dialectical method. There are certain powerful human drives towards the improvement of knowledge in general and its embedding in better artefacts. These include curiosity, a desire to resolve puzzles and paradoxes and to solve mysteries. It also includes competitiveness, the desire to outdo or outsmart others and be superior in some way, powerfully manifested in games, economic transactions and social hierarchies. A third is the desire to live more comfortably, which includes more leisure, better clothing, food and drink and entertainment. This is the thesis of the dialectic, the pushing force, and it applies to a considerable extent in all human societies from the simplest hunter-gatherers up to the most complex modern organisations or science parks.

Against this, as the form of an antithesis, are ranged a number of limiting or negative pressures, which we can discern throughout history. Some of them, such as war, are absolute traps, even if war also often spurs rapid technological change. Many of them are like the law of diminishing marginal returns, or the law of information storage (that it becomes exponentially more difficult to store and find information as the size of the data grows), or disease (which becomes a greater threat as populations are successful and growing), difficulties which through a negative feedback loop, grow stronger with every success. Another way of looking at these is the externalities or downsides of many inventions. There are large gains, but then the costs, as we see for example with environmental pollution, mount.

The balance between the thesis and the antithesis is the synthesis or outcome in history. What has changed with the invention of intelligent machines is that the thesis has become more powerful and a number of the antitheses or laws of diminishing return (e.g. in information storage) have been eliminated, or at least postponed for the present.

Since, in the end, everything is finite, and even the first law of thermo-dynamics (that energy is irreducible) is balanced by the second law (of entropy or degradation), we need to remember that we cannot project the bonanza created by more powerful human-machine interactions into a limitless future. We, or the machines, will hit limits to growth at some point.

Yet the extraordinary breakthrough into atom-thick materials or quantum computing, or almost limitless, free, non-polluting energy from the sun, or the manipulations of each tiny segment of animal and plant genomes, provides a possibility of several more generations of incredible growth along various paths. Whether this will make humans either redundant, servants to the machines, or part-machines (cyborgs), it is impossible to predict.

THE TRIANGLE

About twenty years ago, Gerry and I wrote as follows:

There are two fundamental characteristics of Homo sapiens sapiens which in degree at least, if not in absolute terms, differentiate us from all other extant species and which seem to define the potential rate of growth of human cultures.

The first is that we, as humans, have the physiological potential for intellectual activity which permits us to generate knowledge of the natural world, and of ourselves as part of that world. We are above all a knowledge generating and knowledge using species.

The second is that we have the ability to use the knowledge we have generated to modify the world around us, most notably to produce artefacts which we perceive as resources for survival, or to engage in activities that we find fulfilling, but in which we may not immediately recognise a very direct 'survival' advantage.

The historical process, as it has unfolded through the hunter-gatherer/ farmer transition and over the millennia of recorded history to the ultimate outcome of a species which can manipulate, almost atom by atom, its own genome, appears to be related most directly to these two features. We are the species which generates its own resources, by manipulation of the matter of which our planet is composed, using energy derived from our star, the sun. We do this, always, by the application of knowledge.

What is extraordinary is that when I re-read this in 2017 I see that most of what we took to differentiate us from other species does not separate us from the artificial intelligence-based machines which have raced ahead in the last twenty years. If we re-read the passage, replacing *Homo sapiens sapiens* by computers, it would scarcely need to be changed at all. Computers will soon be able, if they cannot already do so, to 'generate knowledge of the natural world' and of themselves as part of it. They are 'knowledge generating and knowledge using'. They can 'modify the world around us' and produce 'artefacts' which they may well, in the future, perceive as resources for their survival. They can well be defined as a species 'which generates its own resources, by manipulation of the matter of which the plant is composed, using energy derived from the sun, through the application of knowledge'.

* * *

In theory human beings are capable of using a very powerful and cumulatively effective feedback loop. This consists of the following: the innovation of knowledge > innovation of functional artefacts > quantification of functional artefacts > innovation of knowledge and so on, again and again. Each time the cycle is repeated, the process becomes more powerful.

The simple triangle, which also works in reverse, is shown in the following diagram.

The Triangle

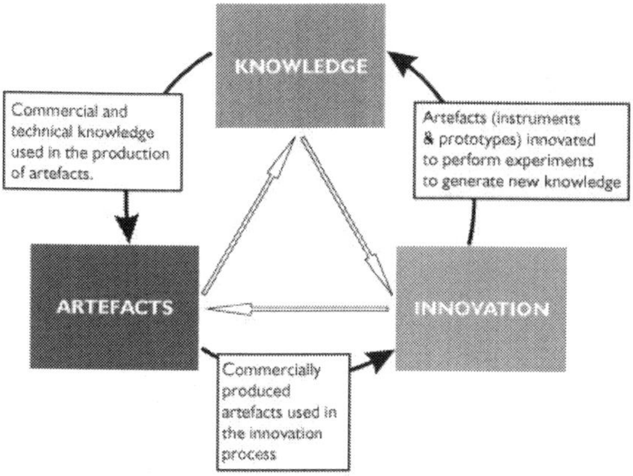

Kindly supplied by Christopher Dawes, based on the ideas of Gerry Martin

Some further reasons why the syndrome becomes cumulatively faster and more powerful may be suggested. Firstly, there is the ratcheting effect, or the enduring nature of knowledge. Knowledge, both reliable knowledge in the modern, scientific sense, but also in that definition of technology given by Marcel Mauss, that is 'an effective traditional action', seems to endure well over very long periods, with the proviso that the knowledge is recorded in some form and that the records are widely disseminated. There are, of course, famous periods of the destruction or forgetting of knowledge, but especially since the advent of movable print in the west, knowledge appears to be fairly durable. In accounting terms, the stock of knowledge hardly depreciates and tends to improve through experiment and selection.

If it is agreed that knowledge has a strong tendency to endure, and new knowledge is generated at a greater rate than existing knowledge is lost, then it follows that knowledge is cumulative. It is difficult to think of any other human attribute which is cumulative in this way, with the possible exception of mutations in the genome, which tend to occur much more slowly.

This triangular movement can lead to very rapid growth if the cycle occurs a number of times. It can also be affected by another property of knowledge, namely the 'meccano' effect. (Meccano is a construction kit; it becomes exponentially more powerful as you add pieces to it.) This means that each new artefact opens up many new possibilities. This is a feature of macro-inventions. For example, the development of the wheel, the clock or glass is not just a matter of adding one more item of material culture. It has a multiplier effect. So the growth of knowledge occurs in a way similar to a possible population curve, in the order 1,2,4,8,16 (an exponential or non-linear growth).

* * *

Knowledge is an absolute requirement for the innovation of artefacts. In the long period since man was a hunter-gatherer, the overwhelming majority of resources used by humans (including agricultural products) have been artefacts, and these can be seen as embedded knowledge.

Yet the non-linearity works the other way round as well. As new artefacts are made, they provide the tools for new knowledge. For instance, glass made modern chemistry, astronomy, zoology, epidemiology, and many other sciences possible. Before this, the discovery of writing had similar enormous effects. There is thus a non-linear relationship between the generation of new knowledge and the innovation of the artefacts needed to help construct the new knowledge.

The syndrome seems to come as a package. New knowledge cannot be used alone as a resource, it has to be embodied in artefacts (including agricultural produce in the category of 'artifact'). The production of a single innovative artefact has a negligible effect on the course of history – it has to be produced in quantity. Furthermore, the syndrome contains its own tight feedback loops. The ability to innovate new artefacts soon runs dry without new knowledge, and the innovation of new knowledge rests heavily both on the provision of surplus resource to support individuals who are generating new knowledge, and on the availability of innovative artefacts and manipulative techniques as the base for experimentation. This simple law of cumulative knowledge provides us with a backdrop to measure what has actually happened in the world. We now have a 'normal tendency' towards the growth of knowledge and technology, all else being equal.

The above account was also written some twenty years ago, but it can now be seen that it applies, potentially with far greater force, to computers and their derivatives.

* * *

If we define technology as embedded reliable knowledge, making things (and 'things' include techniques, for example legal ideas, administrative and organisational ideas) then the speed at which they are developed and embedded can be seen to change in velocity in three broad stages.

For almost all of human history, the great technological revolutions that shaped our world, from fire and the wheel to the domestication of plants and animals, were discovered by accident, and then retained. Like the very slow case of natural or biological genetic evolution, a person or group by chance found something out. The great Chinese inventions of gunpowder, compass, printing, silk, porcelain and tea are good examples. Over a period of hundreds of years the idea spread and survived. The discoveries were not automatically generated by a method of invention that could be generalised and then speed up the process of discovering new and better technologies.

The second great era began in the 'long' scientific revolution, starting in the twelfth century and reaching its formal expression and great discoveries from the sixteenth century in the specification by Francis Bacon and exemplified most famously in the work of thinkers from Galileo to Newton. The method was to make a guess based on earlier experience and intuition, then test the guesses to see which were most accurate and 'proved' to be true. It was a mixture of hypotheses, and testing, which led back to better hypotheses. In other words it was a matter of deduction (from general rules to particular possible instances), and then back by induction (from the particular to the establishment of a better general law).

This is often called the Scientific Revolution and we are all heirs of this unique event which is, as Einstein noted, only the formalisation of what children do when they learn about the world. The Scientific Revolution, only half a millenium old, has shaped our world since and the new knowledge was applied to many new useful discoveries in the fields of physics, chemistry, mechanics, medicine and industrial production.

This classical scientific method was extremely powerful, yet it had various limitations. Firstly, it often took many years to do the testing. Secondly, the process had to proceed through fallible human beings who might either through their own limitations – mistakes could easily occur which blocked the path to something useful – or through the pressure of external 'events' (war, famine, economic, political, religious disturbances) be thrown off course for a generation or for ever. Although compared to the previous fifty thousand years, what happened between about 1500 and 1950 seems incredible in its speed and force, it now looks, from our rushing present, still relatively slow and weak.

What appears to be happening now, though it is difficult to discern its dimensions very clearly as we are in the early stages of a new revolution, is a quantum leap as great as the first scientific revolution, the speed of the move back and forth between deduction and induction, hypothesis and testing, conjecture and refutation or proof, is growing ever faster by the application of embedded human knowledge in thinking or intelligent machines, and their linking into huge arrays of immense power.

Powerful computers and speeding communications technologies mean that we are generating new discoveries and then implementing them in new inventions in a matter of days and weeks, where it might have been years or decades to do just one or two of these before. Not only are more new laws of physics, chemistry and biology being discovered, and technologies being developed at an ever greater rate, but the new knowledge and discoveries can be implemented across the world almost instantaneously. A better solar panel or battery, the application of a new material such as graphene, the development of faster processors, can be incorporated almost immediately. It took two or three generations for metal type printing or steam industry to spread across Europe, but a major shift to new forms of energy or a new material can spread in months or less now.

The principle of the experimental method behind the acquisition of all new knowledge is retained, but the experiments are now being programmed to take place inside machines by way of artificial intelligence. These machines are far more powerful for the specific purpose that they are designed for, than humans. They work non-stop, at incredible speeds, uninterrupted by religious, political or social turmoils around them. The results are then available over instantaneous communications. This is Science 2.0 and it is leading to a knowledge revolution which was absent when I went to my university courses only half a century ago.

What has happened in essence can be shown by one last diagram.[1]

The Pyramid

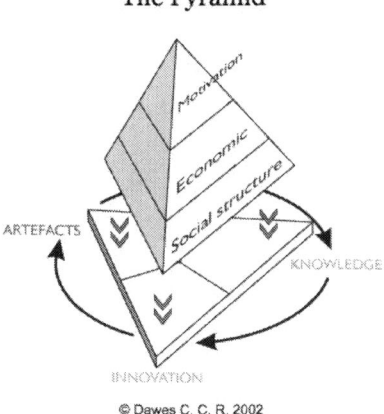

© Dawes C. C. R. 2002

If we add to this pyramid the idea that almost all of the activity of moving round the triangle is done within the computer, we can see that many of the factors which slow down the movement are affected. Motivation is more or less eliminated, for the machine is programmed to go on tirelessly trying to improve at whatever task it is set. Negative economic pressures are reduced since experiments are much cheaper and arbitrary funding decisions can be minimised. The social structure (and we can add here the religious and political pressures as well) are largely eliminated. We can have a smooth movement, perhaps inside a machine which is now doing billions of calculations a second. It is no surprise that the rush of new and more powerful machines seems overwhelming.

---

1   This diagram is taken from HOWARD AND CHRISTOPHER DAWES, *Making things from New Ideas: the Secrets of Prosperity* (2005), which elaborates some of the arguments developed here.

Many of us are aware of the effects, both positive (better televisions, smart phones, cheaper flights) and also negative (the loss of jobs in many sectors, the fragmentation of time and attention, the bombardment with information and loss of old certainties). We live through this massive change, buffeted and confused and I am one of those who is as confused as any. Yet if we can stand back a little from what is happening, place it in a wider context of history over the last fifty thousand years, and relate it to our own experience, it may help to make us aware of what surrounds us so closely and consequently take action to improve the beneficial effects and diminish the negative ones.

TWO

Tools of Thought: Extensions of the Mind to 1936

WHEN WE CONSIDER the development of human thought over the millenia to 1936, we notice certain peaks and long periods of stasis. There is a long period up to about 50,000 B.C. with little evidence of advances in cognition, apart from changes in the human anatomy allowing speech and changes within the brain associated with an explosion, as *homo sapiens* spread, with its characteristic 'wisdom' or knowledge.

The two distinctive features of this thought are that they depend on memory - which limits their complexity both in size and logic - and that they tend to be non-cumulative, as in shamanism. Although there is clearly more than mere performance at this stage, as in ritual symbolism, which incorporates representation as well, nevertheless there are severe limitations. People are living off the natural world, on which they draw for analogies, symbols and classifications, just as they do for food and clothing. There are very few tools of thought as yet, just the human imagination expressed in (rock) art, myth and ritual. This is a state of affairs that covers all four continents and many of the earliest and most dramatic examples are in Africa and Australia.

Then one Continent, Eurasia, mysteriously separated itself off and we have, particularly in the Fertile Crescent, Egypt,

Pakistan and soon China, the development first of all of writing and later of complex religions based on writing, that is the religions of the book. What is clear is that the tools of thought suddenly explode, not only in more complex forms of writing, from pictographic to alphabetic systems for example, but also in mathematics, logic, architecture and art. The high point here is in Greece in the sixth and fifth centuries B.C., but impressive developments are made elsewhere.

Yet, if we take the period on to the fall of Rome, despite some high developments in Rome, in poetry, architecture and law, the pace of intellectual innovation slows down. Roman mathematics, philosophy, natural science and literature tail off towards the end of the Roman period. A good deal of the Greek legacy is forgotten, except in Islam where it is transferred. We have the same problem of the apparent slowing down or stasis of cognitive development, of staleness and conservatism.

Only at one end of the Eurasian Continent does a rigorous intellectual exploration continue. Certainly, to judge by what was achieved, there was continued vigorous life in China until the fourteenth century. Even in much smaller Japan, the sophisticated literature and art of the ninth century onwards shows the elaborate and rich development in the East. Yet, just as the apparent stability or decline of knowledge products, in the decline in philosophy and the arts from Greece to Rome, needs to be explained, likewise the intellectual stasis or non-development in China is obvious. This is well documented by Joseph Needham in relation to the failure to break through to western style experimental science, but one could look at the matter in other ways. For example, one could look at Chinese and Japanese philosophy and art, for example music and literature. What is striking here, at first glance, is that after about the fourteenth century in China, and a little later in Japan, there is a decline in energy and innovation. These areas stabilize in another version of the high-level equilibrium. What led to this outcome, one wonders.

Turning to the West, the two or three centuries after the fall of Rome were not for nothing called the Dark Ages. There was some excellent work, as in later Anglo-Saxon jewelry, but the general level of intellectual life is generally agreed to be lower than in Greece. There seemed little likelihood that in this time and area anything special would emerge. Yet gathering pace by the twelfth century civilisation began to recover the thought of Greece and Rome through Islam. Universities and religious orders encouraged classical learning and art. People like Peter Abelard, Nicholas of Oresme, Nicholas Bacon flourished alongside the extraordinary emergence of Gothic cathedrals. One senses a new energy in the fusion of the new religion, Christianity, with the stored wisdom of the civilisations of Islam, India and China. All this flowered in the Italian Renaissance from the fourteenth century and exploded with the development of printing in the fifteenth.

The early centres of the intellectual and artistic developments were in southern Europe. Here were the first universities and the great artists and many of the greatest thinkers. Yet by the end of the seventeenth century the Mediterranean lands were largely spent as an intellectual and artistic force. This is another great puzzle. Why did the Renaissance in the south run out of energy and turn into the heavy baroque, centralised artistic and intellectual world of the *ancien regime*? Again archaeologists would have been puzzled by the growing conservatism. Whether the growth of the Inquisition, the triumph of the Counter Reformation and the closing of thought were the cause or consequence of other changes would need to be investigated. What was clear, however, was that the artistic and intellectual dynamism had shifted north to Holland, England and France. By the eighteenth century it had shifted even more obviously northwards, to England and Scotland.

During the rough period from the eighth to sixteenth centuries people had begun to use new tools in their pursuit of knowledge. The clock, the printing press, the magnet and later glass were all developed. So was the method of disputation implicit in western law. There were numerous signs of experimentation and exact measurement, which began to anticipate something new. A brief comparison of western textbooks on scientific and technological matters such as the *Agricola*, with those in China showed that a new spirit had entered thought. Yet in essence until about the middle of the sixteenth century, the energy of the development was largely fuelled by a combination of the dynamic in Christianity and the inherited riches of Rome, Greece and Islamic thought.

From the sixteenth century, however, two new developments occurred which ushered in something equivalent in thought to the discovery of fossil fuels in relation to production. The first was the wealth of diverse and comparative data and ideas from the outwards expansion in space of Europe; the wealth of the Americas, India, China and the Pacific, their flowers, fruits and spices as well as their technologies and philosophies. Challenged and stimulated, people like Montaigne and Montesquieu formulated new systems out of the new knowledge. It is impossible to envisage the Scottish and French Enlightenment without this inspiration.

Much of the energy in western speculation, its sense of openness, of new things to be discovered, of a rush of discovery, came originally from rediscovering Greek and other thought, or the discovery of ideas from outside Europe. This was, in a way, like burning up the resources of a newly discovered landscape, similar to the energy to be found in pristine woods or rich untouched soil, which had largely fuelled the feudal production revolution. Yet this kind of sudden burst of intellectual energy was still, in a way, a form of living off current energy, equivalent to the wind, water, animals and forests of the feudal productive phase. The widening resources of knowledge could only sustain a certain level of activity because one had to wait for data. Such intellectual resources could only sustain a certain level of activity because one had to wait for the data; people were, in essence, creaming off the slow pace of nature and its evolution.

In order to sustain long-term innovation of thought what was needed was something equivalent to the discovery of fossil fuels, that is to say a technique which would provide almost unlimited bounty by releasing much more directly the equivalent of the energy of the sun. People had to find a way of approaching reliable knowledge directly, not just waiting on chance variations in nature, or the chance discovery of another Greek text or Chinese breakthrough. A method for generating variation, for speeding up evolution, was needed which would take the searcher directly to the hidden laws of nature. This method was discovered at about the same time that coal became so important, and one of its central locations was in the very country that developed coal, namely England. In fact, contemporaries made the connection, talking of the discovery of an 'unknown Peru' of nature through the new techniques of thought.

So why did the scientific revolution occur then and there? This is a large question to which there are many answers. There were, of course, the technologies of reliable knowledge, the seeing and measuring devices without which the activity would soon have ended - the increasingly precise instrumentation, in particular that using glass. Then there was the organisation of knowledge, the societies and universities and networks without which the change could not have taken place. Then there were the methods of thought and reasoning and mental tools in mathematics and logic, which were so essential. Then there was the faith or belief in hidden laws and in progress of knowledge.

What is obvious is that there was an unprecedented growth in the amount of reliable knowledge about the deeper laws of physics, chemistry and biology, as well as rapid development in many allied disciplines such as philosophy, mathematics, and statistics. Furthermore, behind much of this development was the idea that through a combination of hypothesis and testing, intuition and experimentation, new knowledge could and should be pursued. The world was increasingly controlled and predictable. It was likened to a giant clock, whose parts and interconnections could be investigated by the aid of human reason. All was potentially knowable and nothing should be debarred from human investigations.

From a mythical, oral, experienced and performative world of humans existing for hundreds of thousands of years up to about five thousand years ago, *homo sapiens* in five thousand years had created a way of generating new reliable knowledge, of speeding up the evolution of thought. The final breakthrough had not occurred in Greece, Rome, China, Islam, although it appeared nearly to have done so. That it did so in sixteenth and seventeenth century Europe, the system would in turn feed back onto artefacts themselves and led to the chemico-industrial revolution of the nineteenth century with its electricity and internal combustion engine

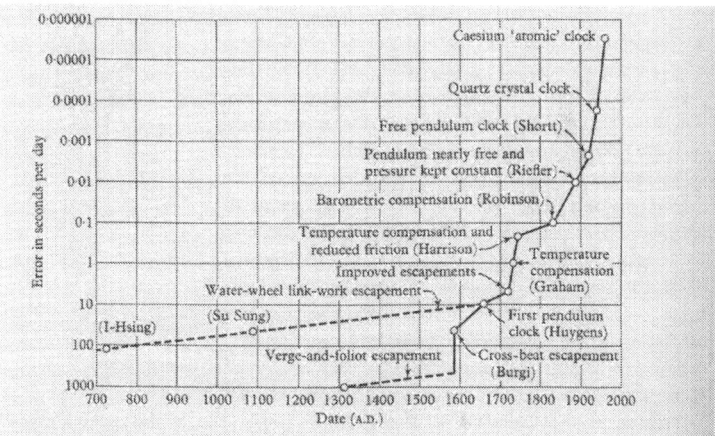

Fig. 79. A graph to show the development of accuracy in hydro-mechanical and mechanical time-keeping through the centuries (amplified by J. Needham, with his approval, from the original graph of F. A. B. Ward, after consultation with J. Combridge and H. von Bertele).

From Joseph Needham, *Clerks and Craftsmen in China and the West* (1970), p.236.

Behind all this amazing development lies improved understanding of natural laws. This also started to take off exponentially in the sixteenth century as this diagram comparing Chinese and Western knowledge by Joseph Needham shows.

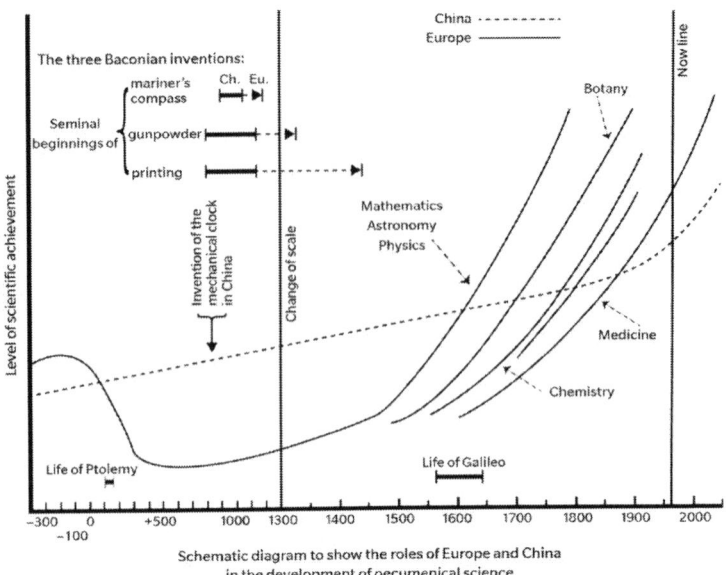

Schematic diagram to show the roles of Europe and China in the development of oecumenical science

Re-drawn in simplified form from
Joseph Needham, **Clerks and Craftsmen,** *p.414*

It would be able to take almost any technology and show similar patterns. Furthermore, with a number of them, in particular those concerned with information technologies and materials sciences, the curves are growing ever steeper. The nature of what has been happening since the mid twentieth century is the subject of the next chapter.

THREE

The Era of Intelligent Machines
Developments Since 1936

IT IS CURIOUS that two of the most important breakthroughs in the specification of what would lead to the age of the intelligent machine occurred exactly a hundred years apart. In 1836, the Lucasian Professor of Mathematics at Cambridge, Charles Babbage, published the *Ninth Bridgewater Treatise*, which laid out how a 'Calculating Engine' (also known as a Difference Engine), using cogs and machines to store a program, might be made to work. Later Babbage, with Ada Lovelace, the poet Byron's daughter and an accomplished mathematician, developed this into the Analytic Engine, which was in effect a computer, though it was never fully built.

Babbage's early achievement was described by Alan Turing, just over a century later, in a 1951 paper for *Mind* as follows:

'The idea of a digital computer is an old one. Charles Babbage, Lucasian Professor of Mathematics at Cambridge from 1828 to 1839, planned such a machine, called the Analytical Engine, but it was never completed. Although Babbage had all the essential ideas, his machine was not at that time such a very attractive prospect. The speed which would have been available would be definitely faster than a human computer but something like 100 times slower than the

Manchester machine, itself one of the slower of the modern machines. the storage was to be purely mechanical, using wheels and cards. [1]

A hundred years after the Bridgewater Treatise, the first Computing Laboratory in the world was proposed in a report to the General Board of Cambridge University. This development is described by Haroon Ahmed in his overview of *Cambridge Computing; the First 75 Years* (2013):

In 1936, a report was sent to the General Board of the University by the University School of Physical Sciences on behalf of the Mathematics Faculty. It made a comprehensive case for a computing laboratory in the University... in 1936 the idea of creating a laboratory for mathematical computation would have appeared quite extraordinary. ... [the Report] noted that there had been significant developments in mechanical and electrical devices for calculations. Not only mathematicians but also scientists from across a wide range of disciplines were making use of machines for numerical work. [2]

Ahmed continues a little later.

In a remarkable coincidence, at almost exactly the same time at which Lennard-Jones was planning the foundation of the Computer Laboratory in his rooms in Corpus Christ College, no more than a hundred yards away in King's College a young mathematician,

---

1 ALAN TURING, 'Computing Machinery and Intelligence', *Mind*, LIX (p.236), October 1950.
2 HAROON AHMED, *Cambridge Computing (2013)*, pp.22-3.

Alan Turing, was working on his paper which would lay down the foundations of computer science and computability. [3]

* * *

Alan Turing was a newly elected Fellow of King's College, Cambridge, who had been an undergraduate studying mathematics in the College. In September 1936 he published his paper 'On Computable Numbers, with an Application to *Entscheidungsproblem*'.[4] Turing proved that his 'universal computing machine' would be capable of performing any conceivable mathematical computation if it were represented as an algorithm. His article included the notion of a 'Universal Machine' (now known as a universal Turing machine), capable of computing anything that is computable. John von Neumann acknowledged that the central concept of the modern computer was due to Turing's paper. More widely, Turing is widely regarded as the father of Artificial Intelligence.

Turing's work, and that of his associates, gave birth to a transformation in the field of 'intelligent' machines, or 'artificial intelligence'. This has ushered in a revolution which has brought together all the huge changes in human cognition, from writing to photography. In essence it did this in several ways.

a. *Machinery or technology could now not only extend human muscles and senses, but also the power of the human brain. It could 'think' in the sense of storing information about the world, remembering this when needed, making decisions and moving along logical chains,*

---

3 AHMED, *Cambridge Computing*, p.30
4 *Proceedings of the London Mathematical Society*, (Ser.2, Vol.42, 1937)

following instructions and sending the results across electrical circuits to humans and other machines.

b. *Machinery could 'learn', that is improve itself, add to its efficiency more or less independently of human intervention. A human teacher might be needed to start it off, but as soon as it could 'read' large databases of information, it could teach itself in the same way as a child is taught to read, and then can go to a library by him or her self.*

c. *Machinery could bring vast realms of diverse information, held in discrete and hitherto unconnectable formats (analogue), for example music, paintings, writing, photography, into one system through converting everything into two numbers, the digits 0 and 1. These two digits could be put into strings of code, which had in the field of information a similar power to the building blocks of life itself. Placed in the shape of a double helix, the four bases found in DNA are adenine (A), cytosine (C), guanine (G) and thymine (T); these were established by Crick and Watson in 1953.*

What Turing was pointing to was the vast leap from the earlier machines for calculation, based on analogies, analogue machines, to ones based on binary codes, digital machines. Thus was born the digital age.

In 1950 Turing published in *Mind* his paper 'Computing Machinery and Intelligence', in which he laid out the Turing Test to establish whether computers might one day be able to deceive a human interrogator into thinking they were human. This article also explained the nature of digital computers.

The idea behind digital computers may be explained by saying that these machines are intended to carry out any operations which could be done by a human computer.

A digital computer can usually be regarded as consisting of three parts:

        (i)   *Store*
        (ii) *Executive unit*
        (iii) *Control*

The store is a store of information, and corresponds to the human computer's paper, whether this is the paper on which he does his calculations or that on which his book of rules is printed...The executive unit is the part that carries out the various individual operations involved in a calculation. (For example multiply X by Y). We have mentioned that the "book of rules" supplied to the computer is replaced in the machine by a part of the store. It is then called the "table of instructions." It is the duty of the control to see that these instructions are obeyed correctly and in the right order...The reader must accept it as a fact that digital computers can be constructed, and indeed have been constructed, according to the principles we have described, and that they can in fact mimic the actions of a human computer very closely...Constructing instruction tables is usually described as "programming."

* * *

Thirteen years after Turing's original paper, and two years before his 'Heretical Theory', the first *practical* general purpose stored-programme electronic computer was launched in Cambridge. Other, earlier machines were either dedicated to a single task (e.g. Colossus and code breaking) or were purely experimental (e.g. the Manchester University "Baby" Small Scale Experimental Machine). The EDSAC (electronic delay storage automatic calculator), constructed by Maurice Wilkes, ran its first programme on 6th May 1949.

EDSAC

What has happened since has been in many ways just a speeding up of this most significant invention. In the same way as optical glass has been made a thousand times more powerful through time, yet still remains that magical substance 'glass', so present-day computers are millions of times more powerful than those which Turing specified and then helped to build, yet they retain the central principles of the computer, as specified in Turing's idea of the Turing or Universal Machine.

I bought an example of the first commercial 'portable', the Osborne 1 on the first of August 1983, for £1144 (roughly

£6000 in today's prices) about a year and a half after it was first launched in July 1981. The Osborne featured a 5 inch (127 mm) 52-column display, (which meant that one had to scroll across a text to see the whole line), two floppy-disk drives each holding 64k of data (one for a program, one for the data), a Z80 microprocessor running at 2.5 MHz per second, 64 KB of RAM, and could fit under an airplane seat. It weighed some 10 kg. It could survive being accidentally dropped and included a bundled software package that included the CP/M operating system, the BASIC programming language, the WordStar word processing package, and the SuperCalc spreadsheet programme.

The Osborne 1

Some thirty-four years later, with the power of computers doubling roughly every year, one of the latest smartphones, the iPhone 7, weighs 138 grams, less than a seventieth of the weight, and perhaps one hundredth of the size. It costs less than a tenth of the equivalent cost of an Osborne, has a 256 GB memory, (64 million times that of my early Osborne), and operates at a little under a thousand times as fast, at 2.33 Ghrz. If we multiply the speed and the store, it is a machine many million times as fast as my Osborne, which in turn was more powerful than the early mainframes of the 1950s. Yet all the machines, from EDSAC to the biggest computers in the world, currently in China, which in turn is trillions of times as powerful as the smartphone, are products of Turing's first specification.

Turing in 1950 predicted that fifty years later computers might operate at ten to the ninth operations per second, or 1,000,000,000. The biggest computer in the world now operates at 33 Peta flops per second. A flop is a floating point calculation, and a Peta flop is 1000 teraflops. Expressed otherwise, this is a thousand million million floating points, or 10 to the 15th or 1,000,000,000,000,000 – a million times faster than the speed predicted by Turing.

* * *

The developments I have described, as well as the future speed and power of computers can be summarised in a series of diagrams. The first shows the exponential curve in the number of calculations per second per $1000 of cost.

INTELLIGENT MACHINES

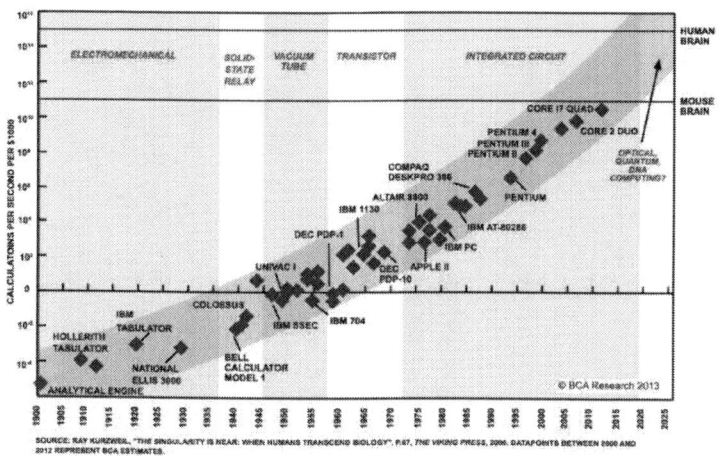

https://blog.bcaresearch.com/
human-intelligence-economic-growth-50000-bc-singularity

It shows the early tabulators and calculators and then the start of the true electronic, programmable, computer. My entry into computing in the 1970s was when the Vacuum Tube computers were giving way to Integrated Circuit-based machines. It shows the power of computers moving towards the power of a mouse brain and then on to a human brain.

* * *

It is not easy for us to imagine the scale of the activity made possible by faster machines, huge storage, widespread and true broadband. One representation will help bring this home:

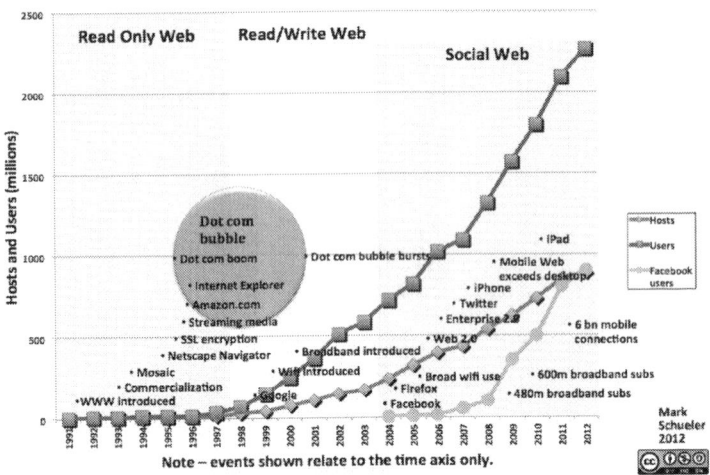

Reproduced from *webscience.org*

Before I saw this diagram, I was not really aware of how very *recent* many of the standard internet uses are. Google started on 4th September 1998 so has not reached its twentieth birthday. Wifi and Broadband were introduced less than twenty years ago. The use of the social web has risen from almost nothing by 2000 to a huge amount now, as shown in the diagram above, which misses the astounding growth of the last five years as it ends in 2012.

Some key developments are worth highlighting. Facebook only started originally as an exclusively university-based site, in 2004. Wikipedia only started in 2001 and its growth has been amazing, the number of articles in 2005 was half a million, in 2015 almost five million.

The vast explosion in activity can be easily illustrated by the next diagram.

INTELLIGENT MACHINES

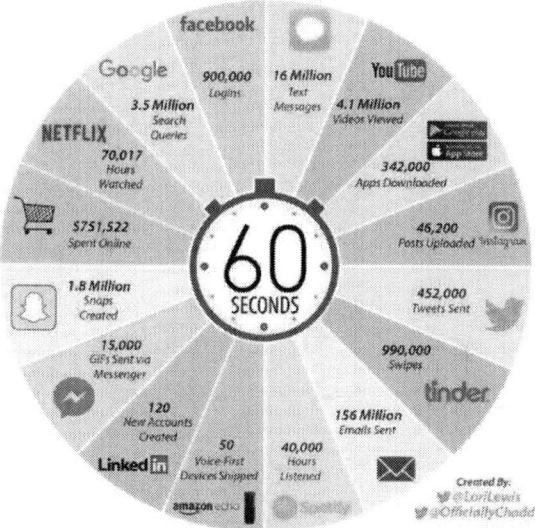

created by Lori Lewis and Chadd Callahan of Cumulus Media

I find this diagram staggering and a useful way to see some of the many uses that are now being made of the Internet. Could even Turing have predicted this?

Intelligent machines themselves are now spreading into huge numbers of other devices which are daily altering our worlds. They can be fitted into tiny flying devices, drones, with a camera and computer on board, and hence alter war, science, surveillance, delivery of goods. After the launch of the iPhone or first smart phone on June 29th, 2007, a tiny portable computer linked to the Internet, they are everywhere. Smart phones of the iPhone kind are made by many companies now, and the Samsung and Chinese iPhones are outstripping the original

Apple brand. In 2008 11,63 million units were sold; in 2015 this had risen to 231,22 million units.

Another way of looking at this is to take a snapshot of some of the uses of the Internet and mobile phones.

From: https://wearesocial.com/uk/special-reports/digital-in-2016

That between a quarter and a half of the whole world's population are included in this diagram, with the largest number being mobile users, is worth pondering.

If we confine ourselves to one particularly significant player, China, we can see the enormously rapid and recent and widespread use of the web. Baidu, the main search engine, was only launched in 2000, Weibo, a combination of Twitter and Facebook in 2009, and WeChat, a combination of many of the separate applications in the western use, particularly financial, mapping and commercial, as well as messaging and email, in 2011. In 2005 there were 6 million mobile internet users; by 2015 there were 620 million such users. By the end of 2016, it is claimed that there were 889 million active users of the Internet in China, around three quarters of the Chinese population aged over six.

* * *

Smart devices can be fitted into many household gadgets to make them respond to their environs or human commands. They can be injected as tiny entities into human bodies to investigate or heal. They can be developed for self-drive cars, lorries and trains. They can be used to predict the weather, control the financial markets and run complex organisations like hospitals and airports.

The triangular process whereby new knowledge is embedded in objects and then improves those objects whereby analysis of complex data is hugely speeded up ('Big Data' mining) is affecting every branch of our lives.

The revolution in the capture and storage of the sun's power that is occurring is represented by a graph which only goes to 2015.

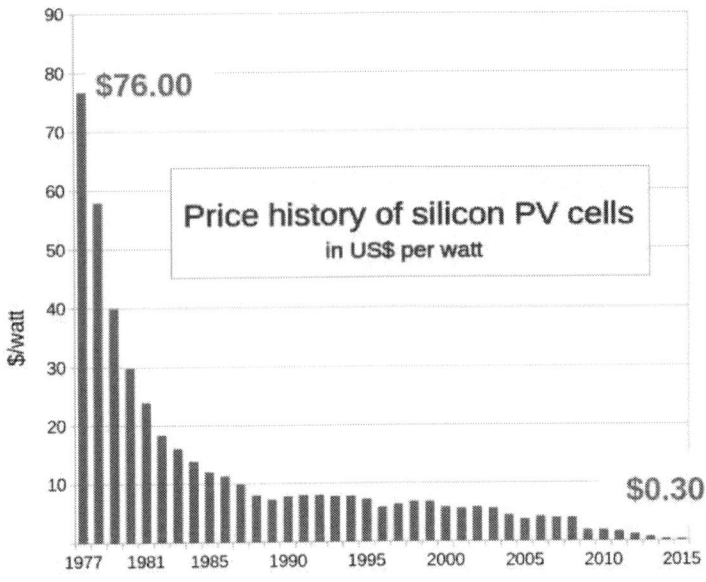

From: https://commons.wikimedia.org/wiki/
File: Price_history_of_silicon_PV_cells_since_1977.svg

If we project this forward, with much cheaper and more efficient materials such as graphite, we can easily imagine that in ten years there will be almost limitless, almost free and non-polluting energy for millions.

Or again, we can see the effects in medicine. Many people now use the Internet for health information. For example, almost three quarters of Americans looked online for health information during the year 2015 and the figures are almost as high in Europe.

Computers are lowering the cost of many forms of medical work, as the diagram below shows.

INTELLIGENT MACHINES

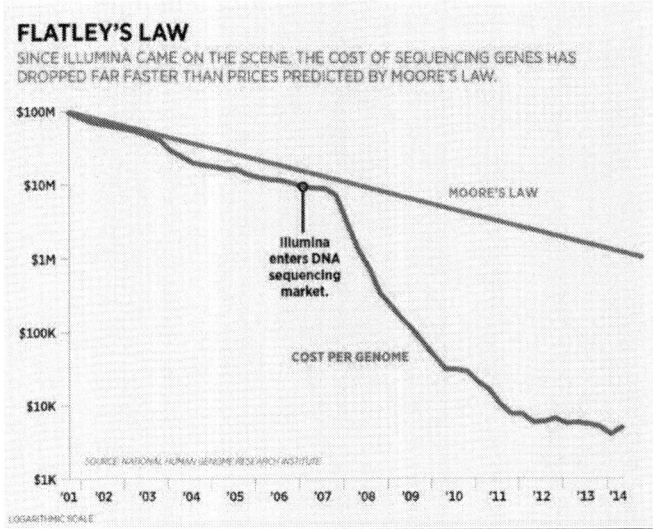

From: Forbes.com - the link is broken

What is particularly extraordinary is that the cost per genome, from $100 million in 2001 to about $8000 in 2014, is significantly faster than Moore's law.

FOUR

Some Consequences of Technological Change

IN ORDER TO try to guess at the dimensions of what is happening all around us, namely the digital revolution, it is helpful to see how some of the most important technological changes have altered the world. I have chosen five of these, with the digital transformation of the present as the sixth. These are writing, mechanical clocks, glass, mechanical printing and mechanical recording.

* * *

The move from oral to written cultures over five thousand years ago had immense consequences. It can be argued that it made possible an entirely new phase in human history, the age of states, empires and civilisations which have dominated our globe since. Writing was a way of condensing, storing and transmitting ideas over long distances, both in time and space. In many ways it was the direct predecessor of our current internet world.

Without writing, it would have been impossible to set up the bureaucracies, the legal systems, the taxation systems, the systems of property and ownership, which were the fundamental features of states and civilisations. There could not have been legal codes, the concept of abstract legal truths, the registration of people and property, the recorded history of past decisions which are essential if power is to be exercised over a wide territory comprising hundreds of thousands or perhaps millions of people. So the State, Empire and Civilisation are the products of writing.

The invention of writing had immense economic consequences. It initiated the separate sphere of 'the economy', to a certain extent independent of politics, society and religion, with its own laws and compulsions. Writing allowed the emergence of general purpose money (money as a store of value, unit of account, unit of transactions) and hence allowed the growth of true markets, where goods of different kinds could easily be exchanged. Money allowed the development of most of the vital tools of modern economies: accounting systems, the recording of debt, the possibility of long-term credit, the transmission of value over long distances of time and space vital for trade.

Money allowed the development of private property, new landholding methods, taxation and rents by individuals and the state and hence the emergence of professional classes and bureaucracies. Money allowed the development of legal protection and arbitration in economic disputes and the registration and enumeration of wealth. So writing turned barter into trade, joint and undivided group property into individual wealth, the state and landlords into powerful agents in the pursuit of wealth and profit. Much of our economic world was laid out in that first transition and indeed it is widely believed that writing was first developed precisely as an economic instrument.

The effects of the discovery of writing on early human sociality was immense. It led to a certain standardisation of interactions over larger social units, breaking down small regional and tribal differences, joining people into large social agglomerates, cities and states, with dense populations. New social hierarchies, including slavery, caste and proto-classes were instituted and a new huge division between the literate, the high or great culture who ruled through the pen and sword, and the mass, who worked for them, developed. The tribe gave way to the clan or even the smaller family, the children of the elites started to go to new institutions to learn how to manipulate the new tools of thoughts, writing and reading. So new professional classes were born. It was as much a revolution in society as it was in economy and polity.

The change from oral to written communication is believed to have caused a massive shift in human cognition and belief. It made possible the separation of 'religion' from the rest of life, as a separate or instituted sphere. There were now a set of spiritual truths, the 'religions of the book', derive from this change, that is Hinduism, Buddhism, Judaism, Christianity and Islam. There was an external 'Truth' which was given by God, laid out in various dogmatic statements, affecting ethics (the construction of absolute Good and Evil), in metaphysics, and co-ordinated by a formal priesthood and inscribed on the antecedents of paper. Ethical universalism, absolute truths, exclusive and competing world religions, all were constructed by writing.

The first move was to picture writing, analogies of the ideas in pictographs or single picture words (logographs) as in early writing, a form of which survives to China to this day. Then the revolution of the alphabet introduced the break between the eye and the ear in symbolic writing. Powerful ways of representing reality and manipulating meaning were encapsulated in purely abstract signs, alphabets.

* * *

The introduction of mechanical clocks with the escapement mechanism from the twelfth century in the West also had large political effects, if more indirectly. For example, by standardising time and putting it into the control of organisations, monasteries, town and national governments, further efficiencies were achieved which were behind the rapid growth of the power and wealth of western Europe between the twelfth and sixteenth centuries.

Clocks and mechanical clockwork from the twelfth century in the West continued the refinement of economic activities. It has been argued that the Benedictines, with their clock-based monasteries, were the original template for capitalism. Hard and disciplined productive work to a strict time regime, the view of time as a precious commodity (time is money), the rationalisation, experimentation and orderly life synchronised by bells and clocks, all propelled Europe in a new direction. The clock was the producer of uniform items – seconds, minutes and hours – on a virtual assembly line or machine, independent of human and natural forces, of the organic flow of wind, water and sun. In a second revolution from the sixteenth century, clocks synchronised production and economic activities in factories, 'factory time', where one 'clocked on' and off. Time became even more accurately measured and an obsession with time is built into our civilisation as we measure everything now in micro and even nano-seconds.

The development of mechanical clocks had other effects. The synchronisation of relationships through standardised time, the new divisions between 'leisure' time and 'work' time, the ability to plan large events, military, productive, ceremonial and social, with new time keeping machines altered the scale of human living. Social experiences were homogenised. Day and night, the seasons of the year, the stages of life were given a uniform underpinning by the growing importance of the external passage of seconds, minutes, hours, days and weeks, man-made yet seemingly external and impervious to the natural world.

The advent of mechanical clocks again divorced humans from their natural, analogical, environment by turning time into something created by a machine, artificial, precise and uniform. New concepts of regularity, of the external world as ruled by hidden clockwork-like mechanisms, of quantity above quality, of humans as subject to the laws of progress, developed rapidly. This all changed the attitudes to the past and present, the individual in relation to the group (each person finally carried around their own time piece), and even affected religion through the impetus to the clockwork precision of the Christian monastic orders.

* * *

Equally important was the parallel development of high quality glass manufacture from the fourteenth century, which again worked indirectly but powerfully on human organisation and perception. Glass enabled humans to use their main sense organ, the eye, far more efficiently and precisely. Improved glass lay behind the growing precision and accuracy which was a central feature of the Renaissance, and indeed many features of that huge transformation in art and knowledge can be traced, as with mirrors and windows, to the influence of glass.

Likewise the Scientific Revolution was highly influenced by glass. Most of the major achievements, from Galileo with his telescope, through Boyle with his glass device for establishing the vacuum, through Hooke and Van Leuwenhoek with their microscopes revealing a world below normal vision, through to Newton with his lenses and the discovery of the nature of light, depended on glass. Most of the major advances in chemistry, physics and biology would have been impossible without glass. These advances in turn lay behind the powerful new technologies, centrally steam power and new chemical and medical discoveries, of the later eighteenth and nineteenth centuries. So glass was fundamental in shifting the world balance of power away from Asia and the Middle East to western Europe for two centuries.

As clocks were changing the economic world, the world of highly improved glass reinforced and paralleled their influence. Clocks, and later compasses and even later pocket watches were encased and improved by glass. Glass improved housing in the colder north of Europe. Glass extended the working day by allowing daylight to come into homes and factories with window glass. It extended the summer into the winter in glass houses for plants.

New and important plant species could now be brought safely from distant lands in glass containers. Drinks could be served more agreeably in glass goblets, shops and carriages made more attractive by glass windows. Diseases could now be investigated with microscopes, and the hygiene of houses improved as sunlight entered them through glass and people could see the dirt more clearly. Navigation improved with telescopes and water-resistant compasses.

Spectacles gave professionals another twenty years of intellectual life as long-sightedness afflicted them in their forties, a condition which had previously made reading and writing almost impossible. Indirectly, by allowing the development of chemistry and the discovery of the vacuum, glass made the industrial and chemical revolution of the nineteenth century possible. Where would we be today without the glass in our trains, cars, planes and houses? Glass is everywhere and its economic effects are incalculable.

The effects of glass on social life was equally great. It altered social leisure with new wine glasses, containers for storing food and drink, art forms, shopping experiences. The nature of the house was transformed with mirrors, windows, bottles and later light bulbs, so the social relations within them were re-shaped. Later, cars with glass screens, television sets with glass fronts altered all of social living. The social relations of young and old were altered as old people continued in politics, law, education and many other fields equipped with their indispensable tools of spectacles.

Glass may have had an even greater effect, for it changed the balance between the eye, which was privileged by the new optical tools, over the ear. Truth became something which a person could pursue below the level of ordinary reality with microscopes and beyond the range of ordinary eyesight with telescopes. Once new laws were discovered, they could be represented ever more precisely with true perspective and the clarity aided by mirrors and frames of glass. So glass, by being the indispensable element in the western Renaissance and the Scientific Revolution, altered the whole artistic, cultural and ideological frame of a civilisation. Through the mirror it aided introspection and the concept of the individual separated off from the crowd, and changing through the life cycle, as in the self-portraits of Rembrandt.

* * *

The next technology, mechanical, metal, movable-part printing was in many ways analogous to writing in its effects. It has been credited with moving political organisations on to their next stage, that is from the State and Empire as the main political units to the nation-state. By printing in regional languages (French, English, Dutch), it created a form of national identity which had not existed before, unifying people into the blocks which have lasted since.

Printing codified and validated national histories, helped national education, aided national businesses and administration. Machine printing aided in every sphere of life with the multiplication of useful information on a much more rapid and repeatable scale, whether in military, agricultural, commercial, demographic or other knowledge, which helped to integrate large numbers of people into a uniform, imagined, community. It also propped up growing divisions between nations, for example between different religious states with the Protestant Reformation.

Equally dramatic were the effects of printing on the economy. Like the clock, printing led to the production of standardised, repeatable, units, with the mechanical printing press with interchangeable parts producing units of various kinds. This is the basis of mass production and factory engineering. The book was the first mass-produced knowledge item, artificially multiplying knowledge and extending the realm of reliable information through education and through space and time.

By increasing the efficiency and flow of reliable, stored, information, printing was behind the advance of science and the propagation of new information which was flowing into Europe from all over the planet in the era of discoveries. No early modern economy of the West could have managed without printed books. The increasing advantage of western Europe over its hitherto dominant adversaries, Islam and the great civilisations of eastern Asia, is related to the rapid development of mechanical, movable part, printing. The development of cheap mass printing harnessing non-human power in the middle of the nineteenth century again had immense economic effects through education and the marketing of knowledge.

Printing also altered the relations of the young and the old and of men and women. Children's literature, novels and plays as models for life, didactic literature in schools, all these deeply influenced age and sex relations. The development of universities and schools, of new leisure facilities such as libraries, were affected. There was a subversion of authority, since the book could contain knowledge which bypassed the usual channels of social power. Printing affected language, not only through prioritising grammar and regional languages, but also through the publication of dictionaries and translations of foreign works. The change in languages and vocabularies in turn affected social relations, not only with those nearby but with people in other countries and civilisations about whom one could now learn from books.

Printing was momentous in other ways. Printing again

separated people from their immediate context, reading a book took people away from the here and now into history, into other people's minds and lives and to distant lands, real and imagined. Also printing encouraged individualism. With access to books, no longer was a person as subject to group or peer pressure. It separated the mind from the body, leading to the dissociation of sensibility, where feelings and ideas were increasingly split apart.

Truth was externalised onto paper, made more certain in inscribed words on a page, yet information was simultaneously open to challenge through criticism and the awareness that the certainties of a past generation were no longer perceived to be right. Truth was now conceived of as linear, flowing along the lines of print, rather than arriving as a mass of impressions in sound and sight in one inseparable entity. The individualism of access to truth clearly also deeply affected the core of beliefs, helping to usher in religious individualism in the Reformation and later scepticism.

In fact, along with glass, printing helped to usher in an open philosophical world where truth was always partial and incomplete. We know certain things, but can improve on them by searching and then producing new books. New truth is to be found, the suspended judgement is to be preferred, new things are to be found under the sun. Along with the mechanical clock, there is a sense of movement, of progress in knowledge and the world so that the cyclical sense of time and repetition is undermined.

* * *

The fifth technology is that of the invention of machines for recording the external world. From the invention of the camera in the 1830s, the age of mechanical reproduction was expanded in the 1890s with the moving image and the 1930s with television. All this occurred alongside parallel revolutions in capturing text and sound and projecting them over great distances, the telegram, the telephone and later the fax.

The recording era shaped Empires through new ways of collecting and storing data, changed political perceptions through photo-journalism, altered the relations of the general populace and their representatives through television and the popular press. In many ways it was, along with printing, the foundation of the true 'global village' of which Marshall McLuhan wrote in the 1960s. The age of mechanical reproduction of images and sounds was a general communications revolution lasting a century and a half which laid many of the foundations for what is happening now.

What differentiates it is that it was an *analogue* revolution - sights and sounds were replicated as analogies to what they represented, rather than digitally, as today. Secondly, the machines making this possible, the cameras and sound recorders, were operated by humans, they had no inbuilt programs or intelligence. The move from analogue to digital, and from human to machine intelligence magnified the effects of these transformative technologies.

The recording era of cameras, moving film and television worked alongside industrialism and can be seen as the information arm of that revolution. Images were mass produced, standardised, recorded by machines, and later made ubiquitous by electricity. These images fuelled the consumption of goods through advertising, kept the industrial population moderately contented in their leisure activities, and conveyed information accurately and almost costlessly across the planet. Virtual travel in time and space opened up with photo journalism and then films and television. The world existed to be photographed and filmed. New desires for experiences and things were aroused. The world became a global village well before our current revolution of the internet age. The new desire for the tools of the age of mechanical reproduction in turn generated a huge demand for, and research into, electronics, radio and ultimately computers.

The age of recorded media dovetailed with all this, applying the machine to images and sounds to alter every aspect of society. The cinema and television altered social leisure and who participated in entertainment. The telephone, telegraph and photograph altered relations between individuals over distances, simultaneously holding together and dividing worlds.

Travel and tourism were both encouraged and made possible. The move from public, participator, active, people interacting with others, authoring their own entertainment and joining in it with others, to the separation between the 'author' who made the representations with a machine, and the 'reader' who passively consumed them, grew. So mechanical reproduction altered, especially with television, the relations of the genders, of the races, of class and age. For example in its later period, the rock revolution made possible by electronic instruments, the new recording technologies and television, turned the world upside down and was expressed in the new feminism, youth culture and race relations.

The machines for enquiring after truth, laboratories, were aided by the new machines for acquiring accurate data, mechanical reading devices (for example the camera which enabled animal movements or distant tribes to be more accurately observed). These same recording devices then allowed each gain in new knowledge to be safely stored and then duplicated and multiplied and later, with the radio, telephone and television, to spread rapidly across the planet. Time and space were annihilated, boundaries rapidly crossed.

The slowness of learning symbolic languages in reading and writing could be bypassed in a photograph or film which could be 'read' by a child, or even an intelligent animal like a dog or dolphin. Each photograph was 'worth a thousand words', and each film could portray emotions and situations impossible to convey in written words. 'The camera never lies', people were told, the machines for capturing reality were objective and external. Truth and fact were more firmly established.

* * *

We are now at the start of the sixth technological revolution, which has been termed the digital age, the information technology era, or the age of intelligent machines. This era can be dated back about seventy years to several seminar papers by Alan Turing. Yet the exponential nature of the changes, which is not a feature to that degree of the earlier changes, means that in terms of its impact, it is really in the second half of these seventy years, that is from about 1980, that the political impact has become obvious. Indeed the period of just over twenty-five years since the start of the World Wide Web in 1991, or even from the take-off of new platforms in about 2000, or even around 2007 and the smart phone, could be taken as the main turning point.

However we date what has happened, we should expect to find political consequences as great as any of the former technological revolutions. For example, the rise of populism, that is of demagogues who use the new media and encourage a sense of cynicism and disenfranchisement. Many millions, whose economic base and sense of identity is being shredded by automation and globalism, the shift of the balance of power to the East, and mass migration and loss of confidence in authority with ever more rapid social change, are feeling the immense effects.

The spread of cyber spying, the instant politics of the Twitter feed and 24 hour television and internet reporting, the struggle to control digital media, the diffusion of power through mass online social networks, the access to hitherto strictly guarded information through massive encyclopaedias and powerful search systems, all these are changing political systems. They are tipping balances between national and international bodies and between the citizen and the state.

The advances in weapon systems, increased use of computers, drones and robots are altering warfare. The complex banking systems, airports and motorways, navigation systems, all would collapse if the computers were switched off. Political life and power relations would change immensely. Every aspect of our lives from credit, communications, food distribution to mass entertainment are now dependent on intelligent machines. Future historians may well look back and see that the changes of the last seventy years have been as great as all the previous technological revolutions combined.

The current digital revolution is likely to be on a scale equivalent to several of the previous transformations combined, for example a combination of writing, printing and industrialism. We are aware of how, in the last forty years, every aspect of our economic life has been transformed by intelligent machines. The effects on banking and the stock exchange, the movement of money and the replacement of coinage by electronic money – symbolised by the 'bit coin' and the credit card – are obvious. If the machines stopped, the world's financial system would collapse. The dangers of financial systems being largely in the hands of machines is obvious to many.

In manufacturing, much of the design and making of goods is now done by intelligent machines. Automation has increasingly replaced the blue-collar workers, as the earlier machines replaced the agricultural labour force. Factories and high street shops decline, home working and the internet economy boom. Reading habits, and leisure more generally, are being transformed with the whole vast leisure industry based on intelligent machines, online games and entertainment through computers and now tablets, smart phones, and game boxes.

Older people are working for longer years, their bodies weaker but their minds still active. Governments are heavily dependent on intelligent machines in policing, health, transport, taxation, defence, intelligence gathering and education. Everything is being speeded up and made more standardised. Three-dimensional printing of objects will replace much of factory production, cutting the costs and leading to ever faster modifications of design.

Just as writing brought in the market, clocks and glass and printing brought in capitalism, and industrialism and the recording media the total transformation to an industrial, global, world, so we are going through similar scale changes now. Every facet of our economy is affected, but the changes are so great that we cannot see them at all clearly.

Living in the start of the vast effects of intelligent machines on our lives, we know how the changes must be at least as large as several of the previous revolutions combined. The internet, social media, smart phones, virtual reality, computerised learning and entertainment, all these and many other technologies enormously amplify the power of writing, clocks, glass, printing, industrialism and the recording media by adding human programming. In other words intelligence of a kind is embedded in all of them, and they are changing all of our social parameters at an ever faster rate.

The remaining social hierarchies of gender, age, race, wealth, professional expertise are being further subverted. New forms of virtual sociality, new international friendships and networks are possible. The world has shrunk hugely, not now a global village but a global household. Yet we are also simultaneously distanced from each other, into ever more fragmented and often anxious and self-questioning social spaces. We are more intensely involved with more people, yet also vulnerable and often repelled by them.

So our leisure, our consumption patterns, our educational systems, our ability to work and share with others are being enormously expanded and changed. This is happening at an exponential rate of change, so that the society of each cohort, even people who are two or three years apart, is very different. Parents are cut off from their children, teachers from their pupils, politicians from their electorate, authors from their readers.

While at the same time the potentials for new social interactions and exchanges, appears to multiply at a similar rate. Whether the robots created with the new artificial intelligence will be social beings, as they clean our houses, stock our fridges, educate our children, look after us in sickness and old age, or invade our countries, we do not yet know.

The intelligent machine, combined with the shift from analogue to digital, incorporates all the momentous effects of the previous five inventions and then magnifies them many times over by explicitly, rather than implicitly, embedding intelligence in the artefacts, that is programmed thought and the possible of self-education.

By adding together the power of symbolic writing and mathematics, the precision of clock time, the heightened vision and high resistance of glass, the machine replications of printing and the mechanical capturing and dissemination of mechanical reproduction of sound and vision, the digital revolution has launched an exponential change in human cognition. As a result, the philosophical, emotional and, no doubt, religious basis of what it is to be human has been altered dramatically.

The changes are so immense and are happening at such an accelerated speed that it is impossible to stand back and grasp what is happening. The previous revolutions took generations to create their effects while the present revolutions occur in a few years or even months. For example the social network revolution allowed by the internet has mostly occurred in the last ten years.

As we watch ourselves and our interactions with the new intelligent machines – computers, smart phones, tablets, game boxes, the internet of things – and hear each day of new and extraordinary advances in robotics, medicine, transport, we know something amazing is happening. We know that we are in danger of addiction to the desire to receive and send messages to our friends and colleagues. We know that we crave for the stimulus of new images, of food, sport, political catastrophes and perhaps sex. We know that we now have access to huge new libraries of textual information (e.g. Wikipedia), or visual libraries (e.g. Youtube), which makes each of us able to investigate the world, whether we are in Cambridge or a remote Himalayan village, in a way which would have been totally impossible even to dream of a generation ago.

We know that the constant bombardment of information and access to private and hitherto concealed information has shaken our belief in authority figures, and hence the rise of cynicism and political populism. We know that the presentation of totally opposed and strongly asserted 'facts' leads us to feel astray in a 'post-truth', 'fake news' world of instant reversals of what we thought was firmly established.

We know that our identities, moralities, convictions are being constantly threatened by the presentation of alternative challenges of other cultures and other histories and that this leads to widespread anxiety, feelings of threat, and a feeling that our worlds may be collapsing.

We also know that our potentials to enjoy wonderful experiences, music, films, friendships over long distances, are daily being enhanced. Yet what exactly is happening and will happen in this new, accelerating, runaway world, we do not know.

FIVE

Living With Intelligent Machines

There is a well-known finding in Artificial Intelligence that as soon as an A.I. device works, it is no longer classified as A.I. As machines become increasingly capable, mental facilities once thought to require intelligence are removed from the definition. For example, optical character recognition or language translation are no longer perceived as an example of 'artificial intelligence'. In other words, the successes are immediately assumed, they are no longer a sign of Intelligence, and the contribution of A.I. becomes invisible. This is one of the reasons why it is so difficult to see the world of machines.

A second difficulty is that machines often work at several removes from us. They are a link in a chain of causation and we do not notice their effect since we look only at the final outcome. For example, as we buy our groceries in a supermarket, with food and drink from all over the world, we are unlikely to be aware that much of what we see could not have been there without intelligent machines. The huge container ships and planes, and the sea and air ports which receive them, would collapse imme-diately without A.I, in other words very powerful computers. Our whole food and drink distribution system, let alone the deeper changes to the growing and harvesting of the original crops and

This is now true of most parts of our life. When we turn on our car, or our radio or television, we are unlikely to think of the robots and computing that went into their design and manufacture. For a moment we may be shocked into recognition by a new device, a digital radio or self-drive car, but then we quickly forget. The only way we would truly learn how much of our life is now suffused with intelligent machines is if the machines stopped. E.M. Forster wrote a short story anticipating the power of machines in 1909 entitled 'The Machine Stops'. He saw some thirty or so years before Turing how the human world would be extinguished if the machines stopped.

With the predictions of the development of 'smart' houses and transport, robots and drones, in many parts of our lives, from education to medicine, law to war, in twenty years' time the effects of a stopping of the machine are likely to be far greater than those already occurring.

We may realise that if physically-embodied intelligent machines stopped working, for example we would not be able to use our computers and iPhones. Yet that is only a tiny trip of the iceberg, for as soon as the machines stopped, we would notice everything seize up. There would be no electricity, no petrol from pumps, little food or drink, no telephone or television or radio. We would revert in a second to a world which was not just pre-1936, but much more shockingly different. Our world has four times as many people as the 1950s, many of them living at a far higher standard of living than then. If we were unable to 're-boot' the machines, Malthus' warnings of 'War, Famine and Disease' would become a fact.

Confucius said that we cannot see what surrounds us most strongly; it would not be a bird that discovered air, or a fish that discovered water. The same is true of A.I. The more of it there is, the less we notice it. There is a flicker of recognition when some big leap is made – drones delivering parcels, robots serving in shops, the iPhone and iPad, the first computers to defeat champions in Chess and Go. Familiarity does not breed contempt but rather acceptance and loss of attention. It would take an immense shock to make even those of us who grew up in the pre intelligent-machine age to remember what it was like before. How much more so for young people who have never known another world before the Internet and iPhone.

* * *

Alexis de Tocqueville wrote that soon after a great revolution occurs, and he was speaking of the very great social and political revolution, the French Revolution, it becomes invisible and we cannot, however hard we think about it, work out how and why it occurred. What Tocqueville wrote applies to the possibility and necessity of understanding the A.I. revolution: 'For great successful revolutions, by effecting the disappearance of the causes which brought them about, by their very success, become themselves incomprehensible.'[1]

The same is true in the even greater revolution of intelligent machines. It is extremely difficult to understand the roots of this revolution, or its dynamics, which are either lost in deep history, or so much a part of our current confusion that we cannot understand the after-shocks.

This is a feature of all technologies. They are invented as

---

1 ALEXIS DE TOCQUEVILLE, *L'Ancien Regime* (1856), tr. M. W. Patterson, Oxford, 1956, p.6-7.

extensions of humans, but then they take on a life of their own and soon we forget where they came from. The same is true of information technologies. If we want to trace back the roots, we have to travel all over the world. The Antikythera mechanism is a form of analogue computer with a clockwork mechanism consisting of at least 30 meshing gears, used to predict astronomical positions and eclipses. It dates from between 205 and 100 B.C. Many later developments may have indirectly been influenced by this, although nothing of a parallel workmanship was discovered until the development of mechanical astronomical clocks in Europe in the fourteenth century.

The mathematics which Turing and all the developers of computing used to develop their theories and programs has its roots in ancient Greek, Indian, Arabic and Far Eastern thought. The machine skills which made it possible for Babbage to imagine and start to build a Difference Engine and then an Analytical Engine were developed over many centuries in Europe, which imported materials and techniques over the centuries from all over the world. The Jacquard Loom with its simple programming of mechanical weaving looms with the use of punched cards, which partly inspired Babbage, had earlier antecedents, for example in the power looms of Sung China.

The computer laboratory as an organisation within universities and business firms was made possible by ancient forms of association and later by the work of great laboratory pioneers. We can go on for a long time seeking these complex roots of the final tree of the intelligent electronic machine.

* * *

When a powerful new technology is invented, it stretches our bodies in a new direction. It shocks us and often has dislocating effects, hence the current interest in 'disruptive technologies'. There are numerous examples of these from gunpowder weapons and the spinning jenny through to modern computers or television.

The usual response is either to resist the new, as with the machine breakers, or nowadays with strikes to try to save jobs in the face of automation, or to believe that the new technology will completely replace the old. For example, it was at first believed that television would wipe out the radio, live drama, the cinema and even spectator sports. Yet what we discover is that while adding to the repertoire of possibilities, the new technology does not often wipe out the old. Electronic books are a current example. At first they were seen as a threat to printed books and hence to libraries. Now the market is settling down and such e-books fill one niche amongst others, useful for certain purposes, but slipping into a position besides, rather than replacing books.

Of course there are disruptive technologies - for example tractors and combine harvesters replacing farm workers, or robots replacing blue-collar workers in factories. Yet even these are not total victories, for organic, small scale, farms, or hand-crafted objects, continue to exist.

It seems likely that the plethora of devices which are linked to A.I. will lie between the extremes of accommodation and disruption. Some will destroy jobs and relationships and new forms of activity will have to be invented. Much of transport and production may be taken over, as will aspects of medicine, finance, law, education and war. Yet people will be needed to direct and supervise the machines if they are going to be of any benefit to mankind, which is the most common reason for inventing a machine in the first place.

We may have feared the effects of the 'paperless office', with machinery replacing secretaries and traditional forms of storage, but it seems that the use of computers only speeds up work and produces much more data which, in turn, needs to be managed by more computer operatives. It may be relatively paper-less, but not people-less. This suggests that there will be a mixed ecology of humans and machines.

* * *

What does seem certain is that our world, which in many ways feels very different in these respects to the one I grew up in during the 1950s and 1960s, will be again very different in the near future. Looking back in thirty years' time, our present year 2017 will feel strange. Someone who comes across this little book may marvel at how primitive were our 'intelligent' machines and how little I foresaw the next great leap, in quantum or neural or implant or graphite technologies which would turn 2017 into the end of the stone age in computing.

In a paper published posthumously, but thought to have been written in about 1951, 'Intelligent Machinery, A Heretical Theory',[1] Turing made a number of predictions. He stated that 'it has been shown that there are machines theoretically possible which will do something very close to thinking.' He continues that 'My contention is that machines can be constructed which

---

1 In *Philosophia Mathematica* (3), vol. 4, pp. 256-260.

will simulate the behaviour of the human mind very closely.' These machines might well be capable of 'learning' and hence correcting their mistakes.

If the machine were able in some way to "learn by experience" it would be much more impressive. If this were the case there seems to be no real reason why one should not start from a comparatively simple machine, and, by subjecting it to a suitable range of "experience" transform it into one which was much more elaborate, and was able to deal with a far greater range of contingencies.

If we continue Turing's discussion and ask ourselves the question, 'Will machines ever be intelligent', the answer lies in the formulation of the question, in particular the meaning of the word 'intelligence'. We could take a narrow, mathematical and rationality-based definition such as that proposed by Turing, namely that of computability, the ability to solve problems based on the process of assembling data (facts) and then deploying these to solve problems by the laws of reasoning. With such a definition, computers may become as 'intelligent' as a single human being in the next twenty or so years, and as intelligent as all humans on the planet within the next forty. The earlier graph, showing the development of computing power equivalent to a mosquito, mouse and human brain in this narrow sense, suggest that 'the singularity', the overtaking of a human, is quite close.

In fact the first paper by Turing built this singularity into his specification of a computer. It will be a machine which, in essence, can compute (calculate) anything that a human can calculate. Then in 1950 Turing published in *Mind* his paper 'Computing Machinery and Intelligence', in which he laid out the 'Turing test' to establish whether computers might one day be able to think sufficiently flexibly to deceive a human interrogator. He believed that in about fifty years from when he wrote it would be possible to make computers which could play the 'imitation game' so well that an average interrogator would not have more than one in three chance of making the right identification after ten minutes of questioning. This has not happened and no computer has won the imitation game, even though computers are now, seventy years after Turing's paper, a million times more powerful than those he predicted for around 2000 A.D.

He then jokes about the opposition this will meet and gives a cold comfort answer to the effect that when computers become our masters (a large leap from superior 'intelligence' to dominance) they will treat us better than we have treated our slaves and animals.

There would be great opposition from the intellectuals who were afraid of being put out of a job. It is probable though that the intellectuals would be mistaken about this. There would be plenty to do in trying, say, to keep one's intelligence up to the standard set by the machines, for it seems probable that once the machine thinking method had started, it would not take long to outstrip our feeble powers. There would be no question of the machines dying, and they would be able to converse with each other to sharpen their wits. At some stage therefore we should have to expect the machines to take control, in the way that is mentioned in Samuel Butler's Erewhon.[1]

---

1 TURING, Mind Paper 'Computing Machinery', 1950

In fact the Turing test has turned out to be more difficult than Turing predicted, and this may be because even narrow intelligence of a computable kind has within it some of the elements of a broader and more satisfactory definition of human intelligence.

* * *

Human intelligence can be said to consist of a number of overlapping types of intelligence or understanding, derived from the fact that as humans they absorb many things other than 'facts'. Humans have to develop social intelligence, how to deal with other humans and animals and how to deal with themselves. This is a vast learning exercise, for most humans will meet many thousands of people of all ages, both genders and various ethnic groups. They must learn through the difficult practice of empathy and sympathy, trial and error, to handle both superficial, transitory, social relations, and sometimes long, evolving and multi-level ones. In this they are using their brains, but also their senses – smell, hearing, feeling, perhaps taste, to navigate the immensely complex web of the social world. It is difficult to see computers doing this in the foreseeable future.

Overlapping with social intelligence is emotional intelligence, that is the ability to feel, both positively and negatively, to love and to hate, to appreciate and to dislike. Again it is difficult to know how a machine could develop this ability unless it was grafted on a whole human body. Emotion clearly does not lie, as we pretend, in one human organ, the heart, but in the sum of the human body. A computer with a translated human heart would certainly not be filled with human emotions.

A human has to learn aesthetic intelligence. Through the course of my years at school and university, I gradually learnt some of the rules of aesthetics, judgements about beauty, in poetry, drama, novels, art, music and architecture. It has taken my whole life to develop these sensitivities, further honed by travel through different civilizations, extensive research in history and many aesthetic experiences. Again it is difficult to see how a computer could learn this.

There is the intelligence needed to tell jokes and appreciate humour, to have a knowledge of the world so that one has a sense of the ridiculous and the commonsense estimation of what is possible, and what impossible (a sense of proportion based on past experience and probabilities).

There is political intelligence, the ability to recognize and participate in contests and power struggles, in a multitude of games, from actual games and micro politics up to macro-politics and warfare. Not least among the strategies needed here and in social life would be the art of learning to lie, deceive and invent truth.

Finally there is reflexive and intuitional intelligence. The self-examination and correcting of mistakes, the pursuit of ever deeper understanding, the learning of the rules of an art or science and then the creative intuition which leads one to break the rules and make a totally new discovery, these are features of human understanding which it will be difficult to program.

Although we can separate these forms of intelligence for the purposes of analysis, in fact they merge. Any truly intelligent machine aspiring to human understanding would need to have them all, as well as others I have not described. This is because in the millions of years of hominid evolution we have evolved a brain with one thousand times as many synapses or neutron connections (approximately 100 trillion) as there are stars in our universe.

This immensely complex organism encounters an almost infinite number of sensations and messages during a lifetime. It seeks patterns and order in these, learning to absorb and reject, using not just what is in the head, but distributed all over the body and through the five senses.

In fact, the whole body becomes a 'brain'. For example, the Enteric Nervous System or 'Gut Brain', residing around the stomach, has been called a Second Brain. It has roughly 500 million neurons, two thirds of the total possessed by a cat. It is in constant contact with all parts of the body and particularly the brain in the head. We have hardly begun to understand how it works and it will be a long time before a computer can be made which works as effectively as all the thinking parts of our body combined.

* * *

It is perfectly possible to agree that if we break down the parts of intelligence defined in a more narrow way, that is teachable, computable, skills, then computers will overtake humans in most or all of these within a generation or two. An extreme view of how soon that will be is well laid out in the following diagram:

INTELLIGENT MACHINES

	Current capability/skill compared to average human	Humans better	Robots similar	Robots better	Time frame to reach next level — Similar to humans / Better than humans (2020, 30, 40, 50, 60, 2070)
Sensory	Sensory perception		☺		
Cognitive	Recognising known patterns			☺	
	Generating new patterns	☺			
	Logical problem solving	☺			
	Optimisation and planning			☺	
	Creativity	☺			
	Information retrieval			☺	
	Coordination with others	☺			
	Visualisation/presentation		☺		
Language	Language generation		☺		
	Language understanding	☺			
Social and emotional	Emotional sensing	☺			
	Emotional reasoning	☺			
	Appropriate output eg. speech	☺			
Physical	Fine motor skills/dexterity		☺		
	Gross motor skills			☺	
	Navigation			☺	
	Mobility	☺			

From the 'i' newspaper, February 2017

I find this diagram hard to accept. It suggests that many of the skills which we still assume to be exclusively human, particularly things like creativity, emotional sensing, emotional reasoning, are predicted to be done better by machines from around the middle of the twenty-first century. The table has no sources or notes so a number of the prophecies may well be exaggerated or totally wrong. Nevertheless it does highlight how quickly things are changing.

* * *

If we are to devise a fuller Turing test in the days of robots and much more powerful computers, we need to broaden it to take account of a wide definition of human understanding, and the nature of how we communicate with others. Since much human communication is non-verbal, in expressions and gestures, it would first be necessary to take the computer, in the form of some kind of robot, from behind a screen and sit him/her in a chair, alongside a well read and well educated human being. Then a panel of judges would put a series of tests or questions to the two, human and robot, and after the interview decide which was the computer and which the human. The test, which would vary with each interview so that programmers could not anticipate and pre-program the robot with prepared answers, might include such things as:

1. Make or recite three funny jokes or puns on selected topics and explain why they seem funny.
2. Listen to selected passages of classical, jazz and pop music and rank them from excellent to awful., explaining the criteria for ranking
3. Look at selected art works - Renaissance, Impressionist, Modern - and again rank them from excellent to awful, explaining the criteria for ranking
4. Write an appropriate short message to someone:
 a. to commiserate on a death
 b. to congratulate on a success
 c. to a child, teenager, middle aged and elderly person
 d. to a person from a distant country or other ethnic group
5. Give philosophical support for certain ethical views: such as vegetarianism, pacifism, hunting animals etc.
6. Tell a convincing lie to cover up some crime or sin

I suspect it will be many centuries, if ever, before a computer could pass this kind of test successfully. If no computer has yet passed the relatively far simpler Turing test, it seems unlikely that one will pass such a test. It is one thing to win at chess or Go, another to write a sympathetic letter to a young friend whose cat has been run over.

* * *

Karl Popper's argument that we cannot predict because we do not know what we will know in a few months, applies particularly strongly here. It is all a matter of probabilities and depends on macro events such as political tensions, economic crises, environmental degradation, which will change all the equations. Yet we can make some limited predictions on the basis of our psychology and history.

Firstly, A.I. is not going to go away. Indeed it is likely that machines based on A.I. will become more powerful and important in our lives. We are going to have to live with it and enjoy its benefits on the one hand, and try to limit its harmful side on the other. Like nuclear weapons, once discovered, these technologies cannot be put back into the box. We are as dependent on them now as we are on water and air. There is no going back to a pre-A.I. world. We can only aim to understand and thus control them.

On the other hand, we know that these new machines are changing all our lives day by day. Like learning the old survival skills as hunter gatherers becoming farmers, peasants becoming industrial workers, we need to think about how we train the young to inhabit this new world. For centuries humans have had to learn how to use earlier information technologies, as

I was taught reading and writing and taught myself to type. Now the tools are immensely more powerful and hence much more attention needs to be paid to learning their strengths and limitations.

Thirdly, since we are increasingly sharing our planet with millions of thinking machines, which may develop parallels to human senses and perhaps one day some sort of self-consciousness, we have to work out a whole new set of techniques and values to deal with the new relationships. Just as the domestication of plants and animals led to a whole new set of laws, morals and techniques to make use of them, so the proliferation of everything from tiny drones and robots, up to great A.I. machines like airports or the big organisations on the Cloud, require us to re-analyse all we think and do. We have hardly started to do this because the onrush of this new world has been so sudden and recent, in effect less than twenty years in its full strength, that we have not adjusted.

This little book is an attempt to lay out some of the parameters, to raise some of the questions. It cannot do more than this because of the complexity of what is happening and the fact that we are in the thick of the jungle of change.

Yet we can end on a hopeful note. Intelligent machines have already improved the quality of life, both directly and through helping to generate new knowledge, thus making the lives of billions of people better. Much of the improvement in health, wealth and leisure enjoyment that has occurred despite the soaring world population and destruction of much of the natural world around us, is due to these new technologies. Yet their potential has only started to be realised and they may indeed continue to lead to a happier and more comfortable world.

The new intelligent machines are unlikely to destroy human life as a whole, even if they become smarter at particular jobs and even if they turn us into a new kind of human, as did every technological extension of man in the past. If we switch from talking about computational intelligence to human understanding and intuition, it is unlikely that machines will ever overtake humans, and certainly not for many centuries.

Computers are likely to develop in parallel, maybe achieve specific results such as machine translation or certain types of games playing very effectively. This is not understanding, however, but rapid calculations. Like all other machines which have done things for us more efficiently - moving us through the water and sky, producing food and clothing, entertaining and amusing us - we can welcome them. We do not need to be afraid.

Alan Macfarlane

How We Understand the World

This book is part of a series of short letters written to young friends. Encouraged by the reception of my *Letters to Lily* (2005), I decided to write a set of letters to her younger sister – *Reflections for Rosa*. I was then asked by other friends to write short books for their children.

In each I try to explore some aspect of 'How We Understand the World,' based on my experience as an anthropologist and historian at Cambridge University. I have tried to put into simple words what I have learnt about discovery, creativity and methods to understand our complex world.

EXPLORE THE SERIES

1 How to Discover the World *Reflections for Rosa*
2 How to Investigate Mysteries *Secrets for Sam*
3 How to Study the World *Suggestions for Shuo*
4 How do We Know *Advice for April*
5 How to Understand Each Other *Notes for Nina*
6 The Survival Manual *Thoughts for Taras*
7 A Modern Education *Advice for Ariston*
8 Learning to be Modern *Jottings for James*
9 Intelligent Machines *Conversations with Gerry*

Image on front cover is an adaptation of Spring (Ver) from The Seasons by Pieter van der Heyden, courtesy of the Metropolitan Museum of Art, Harris Brisbane Dick Fund, 1928, available under the Creative Commons CC0 1.0 Universal Public Domain Dedication.

Printed in Great Britain
by Amazon